Escape the Mind Trap

How to Conquer Your Inner Demons

Ian Jackson

Authority
PRESS

Published by Authority Press, Inc.
2360 Corporate Circle
Suite 400
Henderson, NV 89074
Authority-Press.com

Manufactured in the United States of America.

ISBN: 978-1-62865-060-0

Contents

Foreword

Escape the Mind Trap - How to Conquer Your Inner Demons by Ian Maxi Jackson is an insightful and powerful look into the workings of your mind. This book clearly shows you how the normal function of your mind leads to simple errors that can create negative patterns of thought and behavior. It enables you to release yourself from your wayward thinking and encourages you to confront your mental challenges head-on. Fully understanding the power and influence forces like conditioning, perception and habits have on your life will free you from the harmful pull of self-criticism and self-loathing.

The second part of the book offers you a practical step-by-step approach that carefully maps out your route to meaningful and long lasting progress. In it, Ian implores you to stay clear of the world of quick fixes. Through an integration of practical wisdom, common sense, and real world experience, he gives you the tools you need to engage in this highly effective process of change wholeheartedly.

In this book:
- You will explore the fascinating world of the conscious and the unconscious mind and the left and right-brain.
- You will learn from the powerful examples of those that have already escaped their mind-traps.
- You will find the strength to escape your own traps once and for all.

Raymond Aaron
NY Times Best Selling Author
www.millionairebusinessbootcamp.com

Introduction:

"If you correct your mind, the rest of your life will fall into place"
– Lao Tzu

At some point, you've heard the notion that the human brain is an immensely powerful machine. Many scientists believe it is more advanced than the most sophisticated computers known to man. It is also commonly believed that humans are the most intelligent species on the planet.

So why is it that we are capable of the most destructive behaviors? What leads people to overeat, poison their bodies with cigarettes and drugs, or form other addictions? Why are there so many intelligent, sociable, confident people in the world that are always broke? And why is it that someone who feels highly motivated to change, finds that their efforts often lead to self-sabotage and self-loathing?

If you could change some of your more destructive habits and thinking patterns, you could change the quality of your life immeasurably. But the truth is you don't. What's more, some of these habits and ways of thinking have held you back for years.

The goal of this book is to explore reliable strategies to escape what I call the – "Mind Trap".

It is my firm belief that anyone can make the changes in their life that they need to make. Although change is always *possible*, it is not *probable* unless a very clear strategy is adopted.

Change rarely happens overnight. I don't subscribe to the notion put forward by some popular psychologists that – "change can happen in a heartbeat". Real, tangible, long-term change- a permanent change in behaviors, habits and your way of looking at the world - requires an understanding of how the mind can mislead you. You can mitigate this by adopting a clear plan to counteract it; and know in advance how to avoid the obstacles that will undoubtedly come your way.

Unless you are confident that you can create lasting positive change, chances are you'll feel defeated before you even start. This book uses three approaches to help provide you with the confidence and belief you need to create these breakthroughs in your reality.

First, I have combined my knowledge as a therapist, a coach, and as a perpetual student of – "change psychology", to introduce you to key information developed from scientific research. These insights highlight the fact that, as sophisticated as the human mind is, it is naturally prone to errors of judgement. This is vital to understand in order to help end the cycle of blame and guilt that keeps you caught in mind traps.

In addition, I have explored the mindsets employed by ordinary people who have successfully made transformational changes in their lives. By identifying the key points in their transition, it is possible for you to recognize some of the beliefs that you can use to help change your life.

Lastly, I have identified and laid out the clear steps that, in my experience, are the necessary building blocks to implement important changes. Through my work as a coach, a manager and a therapist, I have helped many people make significant changes in their life. I hope and trust that you will be next.

Chapter 1: You and Your Mind Traps

"If I had to live my life again, I'd make the same mistakes, only sooner".
– Tallulah Bankhead

Do you ever find yourself repeating behaviours you wish you could stop?

Or do you hold back from going after the things you really want in life?

If the answer to either of these questions is yes, chances are you have been caught in a mind trap. A mind trap will either prevent you from doing things that you truly want to do, or it will keep you doing the things that deep down you know you shouldn't be doing.

Mind traps that hold you back from moving towards the things you want to do, sound like this;

"I can't do that because I'm too young/old."
"That's not the sort of thing that I could do."
"I don't have enough money for that."
"I'd love to do it, but I don't have the time."
"If only I had the right contacts, then I would go ahead with my business idea."
"I'll never succeed because I'm too shy."

Mind traps that keep you behaving in ways that you wish you could stop, sound like this;-

"I would give up smoking, but I've got an addictive personality."

"I know I shouldn't get so angry, but I'm under a lot of stress at the moment."

"I know I should lose a bit of weight, but I've tried so many times before and I always put the weight back on."

I'm sure one or more of these will sound familiar to you.

What is a Mind Trap?

Mind Traps hold you back from living life to the fullest. At their most dramatic they can be the difference between success and failure. But, more often than not, they slowly erode the quality of your life over time.

A mind trap is a habitual way of thinking or behaving that limits your potential.

Often they can be identified in a single sentence as in the examples above. However, what lies beneath the trap is often a mixture of conditioning, misinterpretations and wayward thinking. Even if you can identify the trap, and become frustrated or angry about it, the trap still persists. If you are faced with a certain situation, or with a certain challenge, you find yourself automatically responding to it in the same way despite your best intentions.

Unfortunately, there are many potential mind traps. While no two mind traps are identical, most of them are created and reinforced in similar ways. The good news is that when you know the secret to escaping from one mind trap, you have the potential to escape from them all.

To do this you must identify:

its origin
its components
a strategy for escaping the trap

It becomes possible to make real improvements in all areas of your life, and that's exactly what I am here to help you do.

How Do You Know If You Are Caught in a Trap?

The easiest way to know if you are caught is to do some personal analysis.

Take a moment to consider the unmet expectations in the key areas of your life.

Start by asking yourself the following questions:-

How is your health?
How are your finances?
How is your social life?
How about your romantic and personal relationships?
How about other important areas of your life?
Do your results match your expectations?

Which of these areas have the strongest emotions attached to them? Which unmet expectations evoke the strongest feelings of disappointment, guilt or frustration for you?

How often do the negative results you get repeat themselves? Do you tend to fail, or get frustrated, in the same areas in your life?

Ultimately, if you are not progressing in an area of your life, it is leading to strong negative emotions, and the pattern seems to repeat itself, it's a mind trap.

Another way to identify mind traps is to recognize the areas in which you blame other people - or complain about other people - for your shortcomings. Escaping from a trap requires taking personable responsibility. Blaming and complaining are ways of deflecting the responsibility onto someone else. These behaviors keep you trapped.

Furthermore, if you find yourself complaining about, or blaming, the "circumstances" of your life, you are caught in a mind trap. The truth is that it is possible to make positive change regardless of your circumstances, accepting that fact provides a platform for real progress.

Does Having a Mind Trap Mean that You are Weak?

At this point it is important to provide some perspective. Acknowledging that you are caught in mind traps can be somewhat sobering. It's not always easy or comfortable to admit that you have "weaknesses", or that you are less than perfect.

Don't despair. Although there are many things that you may habitually do, say or think that are self-destructive; the mind is still a wonderful work of nature and capable of supporting you in radical change. Modern neuroscience sings the praises of plasticity of the mind, because it is able to adapt and incorporate new models of thought and behavior.

You will soon discover that mind traps are an almost inevitable by-product of how the mind works. I doubt anyone has ever managed to live a life free of these traps. Therefore they are not a sign of weakness; they are a sign of humanity. It takes strength of character and courage to challenge deep rooted negative behaviors. By acknowledging your mind traps, you are taking the first step on the path to change.

Is There Any Escape?

Of course there is. When you look around, you will find plenty of people who have made dramatic turnarounds in their lives. There are endless examples of those who have gone from broke to rich, massively overweight to fit and healthy, or unhappy and depressed to happy and joyful. Regardless of what change you are looking to make, you can find a role model; someone who will help to inspire you to make the changes you want to make.

Even if you objectively recognize the truth of the previous paragraph, there is often a little voice in your head that holds you back from moving forward. The voice says;-

"It's alright for them. They're different from me. I have tried to change before –
I've even made progress – but ultimately I fail".

This little voice usually continues with some form of justification: -

"It's not my fault. I don't have the time, energy, education or resources'

Alternatively, it might sound something like this: -

"I want to change, but…

... my kids hold me back".

... my husband/wife/partner won't support me".

... my boss/my friends/my parents are so negative".

These rationalizations can be very compelling, and there is a reason for that. As you will soon discover, the mind likes to make connections. It likes to make sense of the world, and it can be somewhat lazy and inclined to go with the status quo. Therefore, if the likelihood of escaping a mind trap seems illogical, out of character, or like it would be too much effort, the process of change will be doomed from the outset.

In fact, the approaches that might seem like the most sensible to create important change in your life are often flawed. On the surface level, it might seem logical to muster up enough motivation, apply enough willpower, or summon up enough determination to follow through with massive action until you arrive successfully at your goal. While this has worked for some people, it is a risky option. Without prior knowledge of the potential pitfalls - or as I call them the potential "demons" that are waiting to throw you off course - you are likely to fall deeper into the trap.

To make significant change in any area of your life, it is best to set off with a clear vision of where you are going. You also need to know how you are going to get there. It is best to know well in advance in what ways your own mind can hold you back.

In chapter 2 we take a look at how you might have fallen into mind traps in the first place.

But first take out a pen and paper and complete the following exercises.

Exercise 1:

Take a moment to think about, and write down, possible mind traps you have in your life.

Be honest with yourself, but don't be hard on yourself. This is purely a way to identify where you are at.

Don't edit what you write. Just write a list for about 2 minutes. When you have finished, put an

asterisk next to the three mind traps that hold you back the most.

Exercise 2:

Read the following story and make any observations you like.

Richard McCann's Story:

I first heard Richard speak a few years ago. At the time I had no idea who he was. I had turned up for the talk on a whim. My first impressions of him were very positive. He seemed an accomplished speaker and very self-assured.

During that time he was doing very well for himself. His autobiography had become a Sunday Times bestseller, selling in excess of 400,000 copies. He had a cheerful way about him and looked healthy and happy. I also found out he was happily married with two children. On the surface, Richard seemed to have a life that many people would aspire to.

However, it soon became apparent in the early part of his talk that his childhood, and early adult life, had been the stuff of nightmares. His childhood had been chaotic and violent. Just a week before his sixth birthday, his mother was found murdered in a nearby field. She had become the first victim of the notorious serial killer Peter Sutcliffe, "the Yorkshire Ripper".

After the murder, Richard and his sisters were taken into care. A few months later, he was moved in with his father and his father's new girlfriend. Richard's father was a drunk and extremely violent man. Richard and his sisters suffered regular beatings.

After his traumatic childhood, Richard decided to join the Army, where he was soon transferred to Germany. The troubles of his childhood continued to haunt him. One night a fellow soldier, eager to find out more about the notorious Yorkshire Ripper, questioned Richard about his mother's murderer.

It was all becoming too much for Richard. That night he went on a wild drinking binge that resulted in him going on a destructive rampage through a lovely German village. This was a low point for Richard. Soon after this event, he suffered a breakdown, and he was later discharged from the Army for violent behavior.

Things went from bad to worse. He started taking drugs, and even became a dealer. He was caught and sentenced to six months in prison. Not long after his release in 2002, he received more bad news. He found out that his sister had stabbed her boyfriend in an act of self defense, and had almost killed him.

This turned out to be **a major turning point** in Richard's life. He knew he had to do something. He didn't want people to judge his sister for what she had done. He knew he had to write about his experiences - so that people would understand how his sister could do such a thing. Writing his autobiography was an immensely cathartic experience for him. As he wrote it, he began to make sense of all the events that had happened in his life. He explains how he had had a certain awareness growing up, that all the terrible events were happening for a reason.

Even from a young age he had a conversation with himself that everything would become clear to him at some point. The book allowed him to confront the issues of his past. He found that he was able to use his experiences to help others.

Richard came to realise that his life was about more than the series of events that he had gone through. What happened to him in the past was not reality; it had been a reality for a time. But **he had glimpsed another reality that allowed him to move forward in his life.** It was this incredible awareness that gave him the ability to turn his life around and live the happy life he lives today.

Chapter 2: Falling into Mind Traps

"*What we are today comes from our thoughts of yesterday, and our present thoughts build our life of tomorrow: our life is the creation of the mind*".
- Buddha

When you are firmly caught in a trap, and especially if you have been caught in the trap for some time, it is easy to question how you can have been so foolish as to be trapped in the first place. Through my experiences as a therapist and coach, I have come to realize that there is often a logical reason why an individual starts their negative behavior in the first place.

It is important to recognise that, in their initial stages, the behaviors or thought processes associated with a mind trap have clear rewards (a payoff for the particular type of behavior). The conditioning takes place through the influence of a variety of different people in our lives - such as family, friends, authority figures and the media. But the question is how does this conditioning occur? Do we blindly follow what we see around us? Or is there more to it than that?

How do Mind Traps Happen?

Mind traps occur partly through a process of conditioning. When you are conditioned, either intentionally or unintentionally, there are distinct stages that you will go through:

1. You are encouraged to follow a particular course of action, or pattern of behavior, either by suggestion or a clear request.
2. You identify a reward (a 'pay-off') - either consciously or unconsciously - that is associated with that behaviour.
3. You experience the positive emotion of the reward after behaving in the suggested way.
4. You anticipate and seek a repeat of the reward and the associated positive emotion.
5. You repeat the cycle numerous times until it becomes habitual and no longer requires thought.
6. You remain unconscious to the behavior.

Here's a simple example. Imagine that you are a teenager. You're keen to be part of the 'in crowd'. Someone you know belongs to the group.

1. He or she *suggests* that you join them for a cigarette.
2. Your '*pay-off*' is an introduction to the group.
3. The *positive emotion* is the bonding and the friendships you establish in the group.
4. You *anticipate* getting more and more integrated into the group.
5. You are accepted into the group, and ...
6. After some time you *smoke without thinking*.

What Role Does the Mind Play in all This?

It is important to clarify at this point that a major role of your mind is to help you survive.

A reward is effectively a message to the brain that says - 'now you are safer and therefore more likely to survive'. In a roundabout way, by seeking the reward you are increasing your chances of survival. A simple example of this would be a sugar rush.

Many of the rewards that helped form your habitual patterns were not consciously chosen.

As a child, the obvious reward for eating your favorite chocolate is the taste. However, there are other rewards, such as biological payoffs that as a child aren't part of your conscious thought process.

The chocolate provides a sugar rush, a release of "happy chemicals" into your body that happens almost immediately. This release is no coincidence. Our brains require glucose (sugar) to function. The chocolate provides quick supply of the sugar. As a child, you are satisfying not only your own desire for the taste, but also a biological trigger for the sugar.

Over time, the rewards begin to have an even greater pull on you. It is the taste, which you are aware of, and the rush, which you are less of aware of, that start to encourage you to want the chocolate more and more. This wanting turns into a craving. As you discover that the chocolate provides a reliable and easy reward, you start to anticipate this reward in advance. This anticipation, followed by the reliable fulfilment of the thing anticipated, is at the heart of how cravings develop.

Why is it so Hard to Escape Mind Traps?

In the early stages, the benefits (or rewards) of certain behaviors seem to far outnumber the costs (or consequences). For example, as a youngster, you are unlikely to bother yourself with the possible consequences that a long-term chocolate fixation might have. The possibility of tooth decay, weight gain or type-2 diabetes is the furthest thing from your mind. As a young child, you are more interested in day-to-day survival and instant gratification than you are in assessing long-term consequences.

With most stubborn behaviors that you have developed in adulthood, the rewards that you associate with the behavior have become so entrenched, and so automatic, that they maintain a strong influence over you even in the face of resistance (or willpower). This is compounded by the fact that over a period of time, the number of rewards associated with the behavior tends to multiply and become even more reinforced.

If we refer back to the analogy of the child with the chocolate, clearly there are emotional rewards (enjoying the taste) and biological rewards (the sugar rush) associated with the behavior; but there are more rewards that are far more subtle.

One of the most subtle and widespread rewards for all human behavior is approval. Humans are immensely social animals, and reciprocity is a basic instinct. You learn from an early age that the way to gain things from others is to please them and appease them. For the most part, we find friendship extremely appealing.

Oxford University psychology professor Robin Dunbar has completed studies demonstrating, that an animal's brain size relates almost perfectly to the size of its social group. Social animals are intelligent animals. Therefore there are clear advantages to integrating into a social group.

This is why approval becomes so important. Young children are constantly seeking the approval of their parents, who will give it in buckets to reinforce good behavior.

In the case of the child, the chocolate can help cater to the need of approval as well. This can be as simple as sharing the desired chocolates with friends, or just sharing the taste of the chocolate with his peers. As you get older the need for approval remains a constant. Whether it is clothing, lifestyle - or choice of partner - most people like to be liked, and will seek out choices that others approve of.

A Word of Caution

Conditioning plays a big role in the mind traps that you fall into. However, a model of human behavior that only allows for conditioning and nothing else is incomplete. At an instinctive level, safety is of primary importance. In regard to safety, you seek reassurance, dependability and approval.

But there are other dimensions to being human that extend beyond the need to remain safe. Humans are also naturally curious creatures. We like to explore. In order to excel in life, you have to seek new experiences and information. This invariably involves an element of risk. Part of you desires to remain safe, but another part wants to explore and learn about the world around you.

As you explore and satisfy curiosity as a child, you develop new skills and understandings that better enable you to navigate your way through life. To learn from these experiences you have to make sense of them. Humans therefore, are not just mechanically conditioned beings, but also "sense-making beings". You take note of your experiences and draw conclusions from them. What you experience, along with how you interpret it, is another part of the puzzle of mind traps.

In Chapter 3 we look at perception and how you make sense of the world.

But first, take some time to complete the following exercise.

Exercise 3:

Think about and reflect on the people that have influenced you most in your life. Write down their names. Write down in which areas they have most influenced you.

Chapter 3: Perception - What You See is What You Get

"The great majority of mankind are satisfied with appearances, as though they were realities, and are often more influenced by the things that seem, than by those that are."
- Machiavelli.

It is easy to forget, that the way that you experience the world is unique. Your experience and understanding of how things are, is one of a multitude of interpretations. You know this from everyday experience. You go to see a film with a group of friends, who ordinarily are very like-minded. At the end of the film, it turns out that they loved it and you hated it. Your opinion about the film is vastly different from their opinion. Your experience of the film was influenced by your mood, your interpretation and a multitude of other elements.

Your view of the world becomes so unique because each interpretation of events that you make is linked to previous interpretations of how things are. The world view that you have formed in the past influences how you interpret each new experience. You are more likely to accept new information as valid and appropriate if it sits naturally with what you already believe.

This process compounds over time in a continuous stream, regardless of how accurate, well-informed or misguided each, or any, of your interpretations are. It makes you stick more and more closely to your own world view and makes it harder for new information to be accepted.

Your mind likes coherence. In other words, it likes to make sense of the world. To do this it forms patterns. You make associations between different experiences and ideas. You then link and group these experiences and ideas in a way that makes sense to you. From that you develop your personal understanding of the world. I liken this to the story of the blind men and the elephant.

The Blind Men and the Elephant

The ancient parable of the blind men and the elephant provides a useful means to demonstrate the limitations of perception. There are now many different versions of the story, but here is a brief summary of one version.

Long ago in a remote village in India, there lived six wise men. Each of them had studied long and hard and was respected throughout the community for their vast knowledge and wisdom.

Sadly, each of the wise men had now lost their sight and had become blind.

One day a traveller riding an elephant stumbled into the village. There was a mixture of intrigue and fear amongst the people of the village as they had never seen an elephant. One of the sighted villagers explained to the wise men that the traveller was passing through on the mysterious creature. He asked if they could identify the true nature of the elephant.

Each of the wise men approached the elephant separately. The first felt the side of the elephant and said it was like a wall. The second encountered the trunk and said the elephant was like a snake. The third touched the tusk and compared it to a spear. The fourth touched the elephant's knee and likened it to a tree. *The fifth felt the ear and insisted the elephant was like a large fan. The last touched the tail and compared it to a rope.*

Long after the traveller had left the village the wise men continued to argue about the true nature of the elephant. Each was equally convinced that he was in the right and that the other blind men were misguided.

Ironically, as the nineteenth century poet John Godfrey Saxe put in his poem of the parable, -

"Each was partly in the right and all were in the wrong".

That line perfectly sums up the nature of perception. Much of how you perceive the world is both useful and constructive. But like the wise men, because of the nature of how the mind works, you are prone to error and sometimes overestimate the accuracy of your own perception.

Furthermore, the sum of your total information is by definition limited. As the Nobel Prize-winning psychologist Daniel Kahneman so superbly describes it - "What you see is all there is".

We can't know everything there is to know about everything. We can't ensure the accuracy of our information on all occasions. There simply isn't enough time.

As an old friend of mine once put it, - "you don't know, what you don't know, about what you don't know". Just like the blind men with the elephant, in the absence of clear or complete information, you have to rely on your best guess. And that best guess is often based on your experience, and the interpretation of that experience. It's a process that is unreliable; sometimes this works for you and sometimes it doesn't.

A great way to demonstrate the shortfalls of perception is by looking at the field of magic and illusion. The illusions work because the mind has a tendency to fill in the blanks of what is unseen and unknown. During an act of magic, your mind is looking for causality in the events you witness; but the trick works by breaking the normal rules of experience, and praying on your underlying assumptions.

You see a woman sawn in half, or you see her magically re-appear on a different part of the stage in less time than it would physically be possible to move there. Your brain tells you that a woman that is divided into two must now be in two halves, or that a woman that is two places with in a split second must have reappeared. These events lie outside of normal experience.

The mind seeks an explanation for the mysterious chain of events and attributes the bending of the normal physical rules to magic.

But context is important. You have made basic assumptions about the conditions of the act. Your mind has made an assumption that there is only the one woman in the act. What you don't see is that there are actually two women involved - identical twins - and that the visual cues that you were depending upon were very similar for both. You believed that the face, the hand and the foot that were poking out of the magician's box all belonged to the same person. Your mind filled in the blanks of what was obscured from view and *assumed* that all these visual items belonged to just one body.

Perception relies on these underlying rules and assumptions about how things normally work. These assumptions and rules are based on past experience. Reality is not just something that is out there. You have models of the world that have formed in your mind. And the mind uses evidence from your senses to test whether or not these models are valid. If the experience of the world corresponds to the model of the world often enough, then your assumptions and rules become ingrained in your unconscious.

It is important to construct a framework of how the world works in order to interact with it. Most of the rules and assumptions you make are there to guide you through life more quickly and efficiently. But the key lesson is to remember that you see the world through your personal filter. From time to time, your own perspective needs to be challenged.

Exercise 4:

Read the following story and make any observations you like.

Rory Coleman's Story:

I met Rory in 2010. He is a hugely energetic and confident man. Now in his 50s, he is still a phenomenal athlete. By the beginning of 2012 he had run more than 700 marathons and 178 Ultra-marathons (up to 100 miles!). He had even run the Marathon de sables, one of the world's toughest races, a staggering eight times. As if that were not enough, he was the holder of nine Guinness World records and has no intention of giving up any time soon.

He now earns a living training and inspiring others to achieve their fitness goals. He holds regular Ultra-marathon events; and coordinates an event called Jogle (John O'Groats to Land's End) in which participants run from one end of Britain to the other in a matter of days.

Rory's life now, is vastly different from his life at the age of 31. On the surface he was doing fine. He had a successful business, three happy children and a nice house. But as he admits himself, his life was a mess. He was an alcoholic; with a 40-a-day smoking habit and weighed more than 15 stone (210 lbs).

He remembers the exact day on which he decided he "had to change". On January 5th 1994 he created a simple but powerful dream, to stop looking for happiness in alcohol and cigarettes and to "get fit and live a healthier life". During his first run he was out of breath after only 100 meters. He knew he would need to be patient. He was prepared to do whatever it took to reach his goal.

By any measure, I think we can safely say he has achieved his dream. So what keeps him going now? Is it just the pursuit of more and more accolades? The answer is no, far from it. The big appeal of running for Rory is the ability to stay present. He does not have to think about the past or the future; he only focuses on the moment. It has an almost meditative quality for him. But he admits that the dream of greater fitness and better health is still what keeps him motivated. His new goal is to run 1,000 marathons by the age of 60.

Chapter 4: The Unconscious- A Great Servant, But a Poor Master.

The mind operates at many different levels. One clear divide is between the conscious and the unconscious mind. From my work as a hypnotherapist I know that people are often highly suspicious of the unconscious. They treat it as if it is some dark and mysterious force that should not be disturbed.

That is not the case. The unconscious mind is a great part of who you are and how you operate. It is not a great beast to be avoided at all costs, but an integral part of your being that should be explored and understood to the best of your ability. Used properly, it will aid you in your progress. Left to its own devices it will derail your success. As such, it is a great servant, but a poor master.

What Lies Beneath the Surface?

The unconscious is actually quite deceptive. As much as we might try and use certain metaphors to give us some kind of concept of what the unconscious is, it is difficult to convey just how vast and important a role it plays in your minute-by-minute existence. At any one moment, the mind is processing thousands of bits of information. From the moment we are born - even from the time that we are in our mother's womb - information is being recorded in our unconscious mind. Amazingly, everything that you have seen, heard, felt, smelt or touched throughout the course of your life is recorded in your brain.

The unconscious mind is constantly, and often randomly, searching and accessing all this stored information to help you find ways in which to respond to your environment. It is constantly safeguarding you from potential threats, and for the most part, allowing you to navigate safely through the dangers of life.

But because you very rarely stop to ponder the role of the unconscious, you may often think of it as something that only rears its ugly head at the most inappropriate times. You come to see it as something that derails you from what you would ordinarily like to do.

The Conscious and the Unconscious

Jonathan Haidt, a psychology professor at the University of Virginia, compares the conscious and unconscious mind to a rider sitting upon a huge elephant. The strength of this metaphor lies in the fact that the elephant, which represents the unconscious, is quite capable of overpowering or taking charge of the rider, which represents the conscious mind, if it so chooses. I've never ridden an elephant, but having ridden a horse, I can say with some confidence that the horse was the one in control.

Whether you are riding a horse (or even an elephant), you are advised to guide and encourage these powerful animals rather than trying to control and direct them through force. The same is true when trying to control or direct the unconscious mind through the conscious mind. This is why there is such a danger in trying to escape mind traps purely by the use of willpower. What you're trying to do when you use willpower is overpower the unconscious by a determined effort on behalf of the rational conscious mind.

I think it's fair to say that most of us have had at least one experience of fading willpower. Ironically, by trying to suppress a thought we actually encourage it. The classic example of this is when you are asked not to think of a white elephant. Chances are that the image of white elephant quickly pops into your mind.

How Does the Unconscious Mind Operate?

There are a few characteristics of the unconscious mind that are important to understand. The unconscious part of our mind stems from the earliest developments of our brains. As stated earlier, our unconscious mind is primarily concerned with your survival. It needed to be vigilant to potential threats, particularly from predators; while simultaneously seeking out those things that were vital to our survival, such as food. Your unconscious mind, therefore, has some of the following characteristics: -

- It is focused only on what is happening at the current moment
- It is primarily concerned with your survival
- It works instinctively and fast
- It takes messages and information on board in a literal sense
- It is hardwired by your emotions
- It performs its tasks effortlessly and automatically

The vast majority of your mental processes are completely automatic. To draw another analogy, it is a bit like the driver of the car. The driver (the conscious mind) believes that he is responsible for getting the vehicle from point A to point B. However, once the engine is started and a few routine procedures are followed, the vast amount of work takes place out of view of the driver. While the engine is performing a large number of important tasks simultaneously, automatically and at high-speeds, the driver is performing far fewer tasks in a more deliberate manner.

The question is if the unconscious is responsible for directing our behavior in so many different ways, what is it that prompts us to act in a specific way when so many different options are available to us? Part of the answer lies in the feedback mechanism provided by the body. The body provides this feedback in the form of chemicals, hormonal responses and other signals.

For example, dopamine and endorphins are the chemicals in the body that provide a feel good factor and therefore encourage particular types of behavior. Another part of the equation is the weight of habit. The mind normally takes the approach it has adopted previously as a matter of routine.

The unconscious mind goes through thousands of thoughts and associations every single day. After a while some of these thoughts and associations start to create familiar patterns. The unconscious will start to associate some of these patterns as perceived threats and others as potential rewards. However, because the unconscious mind has so much information to compute, some of these patterns can provide misleading information.

In essence, the unconscious is generating general rules of thumb that more often than not are predominantly accurate, but not always precise. These little errors in precision become reinforced through repetition, and can lead to much greater errors of judgement long-term.

Two ways in which these errors of judgement can have a substantial impact on our lives, is by leading us to either become overly fearful on one hand, or by making us easily susceptible to temptation on the other hand.

We tend to be more fearful than necessary because we are risk averse by our nature. In prehistoric times, it made far more sense to scan for potential predators than it did to scan for fruits and berries. Avoiding predators has a far greater impact on our chances of immediate survival than finding fruit.

Well-known financial guru T.Harv Eker, author of the book 'Secrets of the Millionaire Mind', likened the most primitive part of your unconscious to an overprotective mother. I think this is an excellent analogy that usefully describes how fearful and contained our unconscious mind can make us. The key is to recognize the difference between real and imaginary threats. The better able you are to distinguish between the two, the more you become master of your unconscious, and the more it becomes your servant.

Chapter 5: Left and Right Brain – the Headmaster and the Hippie

In addition to the two levels of mind - the conscious and unconscious - the brain is contrasted in another critical dimension, the divide between left and right. Many people consider themselves predominantly right-brain oriented, by which they mean creative, artistic and spontaneous. Those that consider themselves predominantly left-brain oriented, consider themselves analytical, cautious and organized.

However, this is somewhat of a misrepresentation of how the brain actually works. Although the two sides operate and function in very different ways, they are not entirely independent. Even though the function of both hemi-spheres seems to contradict and conflict with the other, they are regarded by neuroscientists as complimentary halves. Science shows that virtually all mental processes involve activity on both sides of the brain.

It is simply not the case that the left side of the brain is designed for reasoning and the right side is the emotional side. Both sides are involved in both processes. However, the mind is divided for a reason.

Psychiatrist Iain McGilchrist points out that humans are not alone in this brain duality; birds and other animals have the same brain division. He believes that, like birds and other animals, the division of left and right hemispheres helps you navigate between narrow and broad focus. Take, for example, a bird scanning for seeds amongst pebbles. In order to eat, the bird has to narrow its attention enough to distinguish seeds from their background, yet it also needs to maintain a broad focus to scan for potential predators.

This function is similar in humans. The left side of the brain facilitates narrow-focused attention. It builds on information that it considers useful and important. The right brain, by contrast, remains vigilant to the more panoramic picture, scanning for whatever else is out there. When you know something is important and you want to be precise about it, you predominantly use left hemisphere processing. In order to be precise, the left brain needs a simplified version of reality. It needs to focus on the key features pertinent to the task at hand.

It is the right side that is better at making connections. In rudimentary terms, the left side is effective in piecing together the jigsaw, and the right-side retains the overall image from the front of the box. The right side is open and alert (it sees the whole elephant). The left side is sharply focused and attending to detail (one part of the elephant). It is the right side that is on the lookout for things that are different from our expectations. It is therefore better at putting things into context.

This is why I liken the left side of the brain to an overly strict headmaster, and the right side of the brain to a happy hippy. The right side of the brain, the happy hippy, is sensitive to its environment, feels absorbed by everything and everyone around it, and is capable of finding unbridled joy in the present moment. Like the happy hippy, it is oblivious to normal rules and procedures. It goes with the flow, evolving and making connections with everything around it.

The left side of the brain, by contrast, is like the 'headmaster'. It is always looking to establish order and understand what is going on within its domain. It can be recriminating and judgmental when things don't seem to be progressing in line with the set agenda. It needs information to be detailed and precise to yield clarity. It uses feedback and reports to control its environment.

The left side of the brain is primarily responsible for your internal dialogue, the brain chatter that seems to have a strong hold over your thoughts and behavior. Like the headmaster, it can be very controlling. Also, like the headmaster, it can be very convincing. It tends to repel everything that doesn't fit in with the existing model of the world (the school rules). It is like your inner critic, and is prone to recrimination and self-judgment.

Left-sided processing prefers consistency. It looks to justify behavior within the existing body of rules. It searches out references in the past that echo its current emotional state. It is therefore self-reinforcing. It functions by using what it already knows. That is why rumination and brain chatter can be so counter-productive. By feeding off existing experience and existing models of the world, left-sided processing is unable to absorb fresh and challenging information from outside its own domain. It effectively ignores alternative ways of behaving, thinking and feeling.

Clearly, the left-sided mind is critical to our survival. It allows you to perceive time, communicate with the outside world and it garners you with a sense of self. It allows you to perceive the external world and your relationship to it. But like most things in life, what is needed is a restoration of balance.

For most in the West, the world they live in has become one of left-sided functionality. From time to time, it pays to take a step back, to slow down the negative judgments of the left-sided mind, and remind yourself that you are perfect and whole just as you are. As Albert Einstein so eloquently put it, -

"The intuitive mind is a sacred gift, and the rational mind [should be] *a faithful servant"*.

Chapter 6: How Habits Happen.

"All of life is but a mass of habits"
- William James

A mind trap is more than just an inconvenience. The behaviors and thought patterns that hold you back are actually real, tangible things. Once a habit has been formed, it creates a physical neurological pathway in the brain. Physiologically, it is like putting a stylus into an old record. Once the stylus is in the groove, it will automatically play until the end of the record, unless otherwise interrupted.

Think of forming a habit as similar to having a huge number of people walk the same route over an overgrown field. Eventually a pathway gets formed. This pathway becomes the most obvious route for the next walker to take through the field. Effectively, it becomes the path of least resistance.

And that's how habits happen. The unconscious mind, in an attempt to conserve effort, starts to take this path of least resistance, unless otherwise instructed by the conscious mind. The old or inappropriate habit will continue to determine your behavior until a new habit is formed to take its place. But this does not mean you have to be trapped by your existing habits.

The good news is that once you start to establish a new habit, you also create a new physiology that eventually crowds out the old. It is important to realize though that the physiology of the old habit - the patterns and associations - do not disappear completely. They are still there but have been swamped by the new.

This helps to explain why people who have made positive changes in their thinking and behavior, can often lapse back into old routines under extreme provocation. The stress scrambles their minds and they default to the old patterns. For example - a reformed alcoholic who has stayed sober for a number of years - may return to the bottle during a period of extreme pressure. The stress causes them to derail their efforts and follow the path of the old physiology.

Creating a new pathway in the mind takes conscious effort. In the earliest stages of change, the compelling pull of the negative mind trap and the somewhat flimsy push toward a more appropriate behaviour, can seem very imbalanced. In these early stages, it is vital to stay conscious of two things.

First, you need to consciously decide to keep faith in the new process. Stay aware and remind yourself of other people similar to you that have successfully made the transition. Second, you need to secure a foothold in the new behavior. Recognize that even the smallest actions that move you in the right direction will help you build momentum.

Some speakers in the field of popular psychology seem to suggest that it's possible to make wholesale changes in all areas of your life almost overnight. In my opinion, that is a dangerous and flawed approach for most people. I believe it is far more advantageous to focus on a key area to change and give it undivided attention and energy.

Small positive actions create momentum because they give the mind new evidence of what is possible. Even small actions and small results can challenge the existing model of reality. When I used to coach people to run marathons, I would encourage them to do anything that interrupted their normal patterns of *not* running. All the planning and fantasizing about what it would be like to complete a marathon couldn't replace actually moving. For the complete novice, I recommended starting with small steps. A 10-minute walk/jog around the block starts to change their reality. They become someone who gets off their butt and moves, rather than someone who vegetates.

For the novice runner, the most counter-productive thing they can do is bite off more than they can chew in those early days. Running too far and too quickly will cause shock to the body and may lead to the participant being turned off running altogether. Likewise, when going through the mental process of initiating change, it pays to adopt the new approach at a pace that is manageable. The key to forming habits is consistency over time. It is what you do regularly and consistently that is most likely to get absorbed into the unconscious. Also, there is a far greater chance that the smaller modifications will be achieved. That on its own builds greater belief.

Consciously Changing Habits

Although earlier I described how powerful and influential the unconscious mind can be, it is good to know that the rider (the conscious mind) still maintains some ability to direct the behavior of the elephant (the unconscious). Clinical psychologists have recently discovered that there is a part of the forebrain that is almost exclusively responsible for controlling urges and instilling self-discipline.

The ability to make clear decisions is the critical component for the conscious mind when looking to direct the unconscious. Decisions provide the impetus to set off new automatic patterns of behaviour.

They allow the unconscious to filter information in a more positive way. The mind is bombarded with an array of informational input. Clear decisions help the mind focus on only the critical information. Remember that all of your current habits (and your mind traps) are the result of decisions you've made, either consciously or unconsciously, earlier in your life.

Don't be too hard on yourself regarding the more negative habits you have developed. Habits serve a purpose, they are useful. Your mind doesn't want to have to recalculate how to perform every task you need to do on a daily basis. It would overwork the mind if it had to re-evaluate and weigh possible alternatives for everything you do. None of us have the time, or the mental energy, to recalculate how to perform a task each and every time we are required to do so. The bad habits and mind traps you have developed are a result of misguided or ill-conceived decisions made at an earlier stage in your life.

Habits are so useful that there is a part of the brain dedicated to allowing you to form them. This area of the brain is known as the basal ganglia. Its role is to chunk together repeated patterns of behaviour so they become automatic. For example, the relatively mundane task of brushing your teeth is primarily directed by the basal ganglia. It is a hardwiring of the brain that is set up to preserve energy and free up your more deliberative thinking for more important tasks.

The Structure of Habits

A pattern of behavior, or a particular way of thinking that has become internalized, will have a familiar structure. This structure follows a specific sequence which, unless challenged, assures that the habit will persist. This is because once a habit has been formed the mind tends to cease its involvement with the decision-making process. Remember the unconscious does not judge or discriminate, and as such, it won't evaluate the habit as either supportive (good) or unsupportive (bad).

Not only will the habit have a particular sequence, but this sequence will tend to repeat in an endless loop. This is known as the habit cycle. It can be identified by three component parts.

- First, there is a specific trigger - or set of triggers - that set off the habit.
- Then, there are the familiar behaviors and ways of thinking that follow automatically.
- Finally, there is the reward -or payoff - that I spoke of earlier in the book.

As part of the process of defeating mind traps, you need to find a way of breaking this habit cycle. The key is to know which component of the cycle to challenge first.

It is inadvisable to start by trying to tackle the trigger. The trigger will often initiate the pattern of behavior spontaneously, and often, when you least expect it. If the trigger for example, is stress or anxiety, this isn't something you can avoid 100 percent of the time. Trying to break the habit cycle by focusing on the trigger leaves you exposed to the possibility of slipping back in to old behaviors.

Likewise, it may be counter-productive to try to ignore or suppress the reward. The unconscious mind may have become strongly attached to the reward, which is essential if the body is sending out bio-chemical signals that reinforce it. By trying to break the habit cycle by challenging the reward part of the cycle, the conscious mind is looking to compete directly with the unconscious; and unfortunately the unconscious will compete fiercely to try and override it.

That leaves only the automatic behaviour or thought pattern. That is the part of the cycle you need to focus on. You need to consciously and deliberately replace old behaviours and ways of thinking with new and more appropriate ones. The challenge is to find appropriate patterns that are realistic to implement.

By clearly identifying both the triggers and the payoffs off mind traps, you will know exactly where and when you should implement the new behaviors. The key to being able to pinpoint these markers is by becoming more conscious and aware. I will expand on this subject in the second part of the book.

Chapter 7: A World of Possibility - Where the Mind Goes, Everything Follows.

What would you rather be: the master or the student?

How you answer this question may indicate whether you approach life with a 'closed' or an 'open' mind. Many people wish that they had already *mastered* the challenges that lie ahead of them. It feels good to be in control, to be on top of things and to have the confidence to know that you're going to succeed. However, I believe that this concept of mastery is a bit of a myth.

Part of the trick to escaping mind traps is to realize that you never truly master anything. The secret lies in remaining open to the possibility of change. Accepting that change is an inevitable part of life allows you to move beyond self-imposed labels and identities. Your life is not defined by who or what you've become at any given moment, but by what you are becoming each day.

This open mindset is crucial. It helps you to look beyond natural talents, existing abilities and dominant personality traits, and instead be open to the possibility of learning and adapting. An open mindset is one that is willing to seek out challenge for its own sake. It is a belief system that is focused on what is possible, rather than what is likely.

The closed mindset, on the other hand, makes an assessment of your life at any one particular moment in time and treats this snapshot as if it is a reflection of your true self. Whatever your short-comings may be at the moment, see if this is true for you. Do you project your current set of circumstances into the future? Are you assuming that things will automatically follow the same path that they are following at the moment? Are you resistant to change?

Be conscious of the fact that a closed mind shuts you off from the potential that you will succeed in what you want to achieve. With a closed mindset failure becomes an identity and not just an outcome. If you are weighed down with a closed mind, the chances are that you constantly justify your negative thoughts, feelings and behaviors. These justifications work to protect your self-esteem, and they help keep your ego intact. They allow you to avoid doing the work of repairing the so-called failures.

It is only with an open mind that you will have the resources to learn from and repair these failures. In essence, open-mindedness is a way of treating your life as if you are the perpetual student always willing to learn. It brings its own rewards. It doesn't demand that you must already be successful, accomplished and perfect in everything that you're striving for. It allows you to be more compassionate and accepting of yourself. An open-minded approach to thinking allows effort and endeavor to be rewarded. Once effort and endeavor are valued as much as accomplishment, you'll feel more determined.

It is this effort of changing that someone with a closed mind fears most. While the *student* accepts the need to learn, work, discover and adapt, the *master* may have an elevated sense of self that is hard to live up to. Open-mindedness, therefore, is better suited to allowing you to embrace challenge, absorb lessons and move forward with renewed effort.

Learn to Love the Process of Change

The ability to enjoy the journey and not to obsess about the destination is something I learned from watching my players during my time coaching tennis. In the discipline of sports psychology, the practitioners differentiate between the types of goals their athletes should aspire to. They have discovered that a player that is purely focused on winning will often fail. By contrast, the player who is focused on adapting and improving their game often has more success.

The goals of the athlete are broken down into three different categories. The overall goal, and the one that most athletes aspire to, is known as the **outcome** goal. These outcome goals may include winning a medal, winning the competition or attaining a certain level within the sport.

The smaller steps and the intermediate results that happen, en-route to the outcome goal, are known as **procedure** goals. All the things the athlete does on a day-to-day, hour-to-hour, and moment-by-moment basis are known as the **process** goals.

Regardless of whether you enjoy sport or not, these categories represent a useful focus for attention with regard to the aims, wishes and dreams you have for your life. When you're trying to escape a mind trap your **outcome goal** is the main target, or the change you ultimately want. Of course, it can also be the thing that you want to stop, such as not smoking, not drinking or not gambling. In either case, the outcome goal is the final destination. More often than not, it is the goal that you focus on more than any other. Not achieving the outcome goal can become your main source of frustration, doubt and negativity.

One step down from outcome goals is **procedure goals.** These are the benchmarks and the milestones by which you measure your progress towards the big goal. For example, if you were looking to lose weight, and wanted to lose 24lbs in 12 weeks, then the procedure goals may be to lose two pounds by the end of week one, a total of four pounds by the end of week two and so on until you reach your outcome.

The outcome goals are there to help keep you motivated and directed. The procedures goals are there to measure progress and to adapt and re-adjust where necessary. But the most instrumental goals in your progress are **process goals.**

For the athlete, process goals are there to ensure that they are aware of how their rituals and routines affect their progress toward the bigger goals. In tennis, for example, process goals are usually focused on a particular skill, be it physical (keeping the racquet head below the ball on a groundstroke) or psychological (relaxing, focusing or maintaining a positive attitude).

One of the key differences between the elite player and the novice in sport is this: the elite player is able to direct focus mostly toward process goals and stays present in the moment. The novice on the other hand, directs more attention towards winning or losing (success or failure), and starts to lose sight of the fundamentals of the game, which ironically are the very things that determine the level of success in the first place.

This ability to focus more on process than outcome is crucial for implementing long-term and effective change in all walks of life. It allows you to remain more open-minded. It frees you to place more value on what you're doing in the moment regardless of results. Putting more emphasis on process also frees your mind to face problems as they occur and builds in the flexibility needed to map out a new course of action when appropriate.

Having, Doing and Being

Another way of describing outcome, performance and process goals is in terms of what you want to *have*, what you need to *do* and who you need to *be* in order to make the changes you are looking for. Focusing all, or most, of your attention on what you want to have leads to closed mindedness. Ultimately, it is a binary equation. You either get what you want or you don't. Focusing purely on the outcome reduces the level of control that you feel over your situation. It sets the mind up to experience failure. It only allows you to experience positive feelings when you have accomplished the long-term success. Any experience that isn't in line with achieving that ultimate outcome becomes associated with failure.

Focusing more attention on the process, however, allows you to remain more open-minded. It frees you to value what you are doing in the moment. It enables you to remain more positive. It allows you to be more in control on an ongoing basis, recognizing the small accomplishments that are assisting you in escaping mind traps.

Be Curious

I believe that people are born curious. As infants this curiosity is evident. Once a small child can crawl and walk, they are in to everything. Their day-to-day living becomes about exploring, experimenting and discovering. It is this curiosity that allows their minds to develop. By encountering new situations and new experiences, the brain makes millions of new synaptic connections that help it to make sense of all the information that surrounds them.

For me, open-mindedness thrives in a spirit of curiosity. As an adult, you often lose that spirit of exploration and become confined to the pre-set limits of your adopted identity. But escaping mind traps requires you open up the mind and become curious once more. It requires that you become open to the possibility of more resourceful ways of thinking, feeling and behaving. With an open mind, success is defined as doing your best. It involves rediscovering a youthful curiosity and being prepared and willing to do the work to change.

I invite you to become a student again, and stop thinking that you should have mastered everything already. As a student, you'll treat set backs as wake-up calls to adjust your behavior and routine ways of thinking and feeling.

Chapter 8: Opting for Optimism - Realism is Over-rated

"Treat people as if they were what they should be, and help them become what they are capable of becoming".
- Goethe

Optimism is traditionally viewed with respect to how things will turn out in the future. In everyday language, optimistic people believe things will work out for the best. As we know, the optimist sees the glass as half full, while the pessimist sees the glass as half empty. But how is an opinion about how things will turn out in the future, related to what already exists?

Although your level of optimism determines how you behave in the future, what actually matters is how you interpret events that have already happened. In psychologist's Martin Selignam's classic work on the subject, - 'Learned Optimism', he explains the fundamental differences between the optimist and the pessimist.

If you are generally pessimistic you tend to view the bad events that happen in your life as things that will have a lasting effect. As a pessimist, you also believe that these bad events will affect many other areas of your life. To make matters worse, as a pessimist, you tend to lay the blame for these bad events firmly on yourself.

If you are generally optimistic, however, you see the problems of life as something that will pass and as challenges that are only temporary.

You view these challenges as something that are only relevant to your current situation and not something that will have a negative impact on the rest of your life. You don't blame yourself for the negative or adverse events that occur in your life.

These are obviously the two extremes. None of us are 100 percent optimistic or pessimistic.

Whether you respond to life as a pessimist or optimist can have a crucial impact on whether or not you can make real, long-lasting and meaningful change. Unfortunately and alarmingly, the proportion of pessimist has grown in the last few decades.

This may be because it is easy to be overwhelmed by the dazzling array of choices available in the modern world. Confronted with so many possibilities, it isn't always easy to know which options to choose or to know whether your choices are right or wrong. As such, it is easy to end up suffering from what is commonly known as paralysis by analysis, an inability to make decisions or choices that result in a feeling of being stuck.

Alternatively, you may feel like you are constantly making wrong decisions and missing out on opportunities. Either way, you start to feel less in control of your life. The good news is that pessimism is now viewed as escapable. As Seligman says, - "*Optimism is a learnable skill*'. Through changing the way that you habitually think about what has happened to you, you can slowly but surely increase your levels of optimism.

For me the qualities of optimism and pessimism have compounding consequences. Optimism leads to more optimism in the future, while initial pessimism leads to more harmful pessimism in the future. In fact, repeated pessimism can lead you toward feelings of helplessness. It creates a belief that it doesn't matter what you do because what you do won't change what happens in your life. And although this feeling of helplessness may not affect all areas of your life, it can have a crippling effect in relation to important aspects of your life that you are trying to change. Here again Seligman provides words of comfort. As he says in *Learned Optimism*, this state of mind doesn't have to stay with you.

"Habits of thinking need not be forever. One of the most significant findings in psychology is that individuals can choose the way they think".

Like Seligman, I truly believe that real and permanent change requires more than just a burning desire and the knowledge of how to change. Optimism is the fuel that will keep the flame of desire burning. Truly knowing why you want to change creates desire. Acquiring the knowledge and skills you need, will give you an insight into how to change. But it is optimism - the belief that you are capable of change - that provides the vital link in the chain.

Cultivating Optimism

How is it possible to grow your personal level of optimism? As I mentioned earlier, we all have a little voice in our heads. It is how you manage the conversation with this little voice that helps you manage your level of optimism. The way in which you explain the good and bad events that happen in your life, has a dramatic effect on your level of optimism.

When a mind trap occurs, it is safe to assume that at least some level of pessimism is associated with it. You feel trapped either because you see the situation as permanent, personal or pervasive. If this pessimism becomes stronger, the trap seems to be inescapable and the temptation to give up becomes overwhelming. It is crucial to be aware that much of the pessimism is based on the interpretation of past experience.

The conversation in your head will probably sound something like this;-

"I tried and I failed. I tried again and I failed again. I tried once more and I still failed".

Each subsequent failure is taken as an indication that your efforts are futile, and it creates an expectation that any future effort will only be rewarded with more failure.

The truth is that these traps are not inescapable. In the trap, you are limited by the knowledge and experience that is available to you. Just like the blind men and the elephant, you're only responding to events from your limited perspective, from what is available inside your box.

In order to move forward and create a new level of optimism, you need to look outside the box and find examples of people who have succeeded where you have failed in the past.

I talked earlier about the impact conditioning can have in the formulation of your mind traps. I explained that although many of your ways of thinking will have been affected by your environment, the influences and resulting payoffs you experienced do not create the complete picture. It is also important to factor in how you personally account for and explain the resulting behaviors. The way in which you explain any of your behaviors will depend to a large extent on how valuable you think you are and whether you consider yourself deserving of the good things that happen to you.

The truth is you are as worthy of having good things happen in your life as anyone else, regardless of what you may have done or what may have happened to you in the past. Coming to terms with this fundamental truth is critical to cultivating optimism.

I remember listening to a recorded interview with a self-made billionaire named Bill Bartmann. He was part of a large family and was bought up in poverty. When he was asked the single most important quality to work on to enable someone to create wealth, he said self-esteem. Sense of self-worth and a healthy level of self-esteem strongly influence how optimistic you feel in all areas of your life. The critical first step in preventing damage to your self-esteem is to avoid directly blaming yourself for things that haven't gone well in your life. In order to sustain the level of optimism that is essential to see you through the necessary changes in your life, it is important to start believing in your own value.

A healthy self-esteem is the starting point for creating hope, and hope is the cornerstone of optimism. When analyzing individuals and scoring them on various personality factors during psychological tests, Seligman discovered "that no other single score is as important as the hope score". As Bill Bartmann said during his interview, what we all need is "something to do, someone to love and something to be hopeful for"'.

So where does hope fit into the equation? How can you free your mind to be hopeful that real change is achievable? Hope is fundamentally the degree to which you believe that your behavior will have a meaningful impact on the results in your life. There are two very distinct ways in which to foster hope in your life.

The first way to strengthen hope is through "faith references". This is when you look at the accomplishments and achievements of others and realize what they have managed to do is achievable for you. You must believe that what is possible for others can be possible for you. By understanding the beliefs and actions that they took to achieve their aims, you can have faith, that if you adopt a similar process it will work for you too. To have faith you have to believe in the possibility of a positive outcome in the absence of any existing tangible proof. That is why optimism is such a critical part of the change process.

The second way to strengthen hope is by experiencing how your efforts can have an impact on your results. To start building hope it is necessary to take action and adopt new behaviors. Contrary to what some popular psychology may advise, I believe that these new actions needn't be dramatic changes in your behavior. Small actions and little changes will start to create momentum. Take baby steps, and start experiencing a new reality.

Dick and Rick Hoyt's Story:

By the time Dick Hoyt had hit 70, he had established himself as a phenomenal endurance athlete. Over the previous 33 years, he had competed in more than a 1,000 road races and triathlons. He had run the notoriously challenging Boston Marathon 28 times. His personal best for a marathon is a staggering 2:40:47. Anyone that has ever run a marathon knows how impressive that is.

Dick's efforts have been accompanied by a long list of awards. His efforts in triathlons have earned him a place in the Ironman Hall of

Fame and led to him winning the Triathlon Strength and Courage Award. I suspect, however, that some of his other awards bring him even more pride. He has won the Father and Son of the Year Award, Parenting Award and an Exemplary Father Award.

Dick never competes alone. He enters every event as a team with his son, Rick. They are known as Team Hoyt. Remarkably, it was Rick who inspired Dick to begin his athletic endeavours all those years ago.

Rick wasn't like every other child. As a result of oxygen deprivation to Rick's brain at birth, he was diagnosed as a spastic quadriplegic with cerebral palsy. As a result, Rick wasn't able to walk or talk. Specialist were so taken aback by Rick's condition, that they advised his parents to institutionalize their son because they thought he was highly unlikely to live a normal life.

But Rick's parents saw things differently. They had noticed something in their son. They saw how his eyes would follow them around the room whenever they moved about. They believed in their son and wanted people to see beyond Rick's physical limitations. They were determined that Rick would have as normal an upbringing as possible.

Their faith in their son proved founded. They started to teach Rick the alphabet, and a few basic words. In 1972, they invested $5,000 in a computerised device that allowed Rick to spell out words by selecting letters with a cursor that was connected to a headpiece. Rick was able to choose each letter by tapping the headpiece against his wheelchair. The system was slow and required a lot of patience, but Rick loved it.

The device enabled Rick to communicate more easily and progress much further. He was finally admitted into school at the age of 13. A few years later, in the spring of 1977, Rick heard about a lacrosse player who had been paralyzed in a car accident. His heart went out to him, and he was determined to do something to help. He asked his father if they could enter a 5-mile benefit run in order to show their support.

Although Dick was a former Marine, he was approaching middle age and wasn't in the shape he once was. Pushing his son around the 5-mile course in a rudimentary wheelchair was an exhausting challenge. So much so that Dick was "pissing blood" for the next week. But Rick's reaction was all that Dick needed to inspire him for the next three decades. Dick had loved the experience and tapped on his computer:

"Dad, when I'm running, it feels like I'm not handicapped anymore"

Watch their inspirational video, and read more about Team Hoyt at http://www.teamhoyt.com/

Chapter 9: Facing Up to Fear.

"Expose yourself to your deepest fear, after that fear has no power and the fear of freedom shrinks and vanishes. You are free."
- Jim Morrison.

What is Fear? And Why is it So Destructive?

Fear is an emotional response to a "perceived" threat.

Fear causes you to resist or move away from the specific thing that provoked the response. Interestingly, the definition of fear contains the word "perceived". It is not important to the unconscious mind whether the situation represents a real or imaginary danger. If you interpret a situation as dangerous for whatever reason, it will evoke a fearful response.

What's more, many fearful emotional responses may have been triggered initially by a very specific and often very real threat. However, the mind has a tendency to generalize fears. In other words, the mind has the potential to interpret a real danger in one specific experience and recall it when any similar but not identical experience occurs. The mind will trigger fear in any other experience that seems similar or associated to the original experience.

Let me give you an example. When I was a child, our family decided to take in a dog named Clem. For the first few hours in his new home, he interacted happily with my brother, sisters, and mother. But when my father - an army officer - arrived home that evening, Clem became immediately fearful and started growling and acting aggressively towards him. We were somewhat bemused by the dog's response.

We later discovered that Clem had been mistreated by his former owner who was in the army.

He would growl and bark at any stranger that was dressed in an army uniform. The uniform had become the trigger for the fearful response from Clem for very real and valid reasons. But this trigger had become generalized and caused unwarranted fear on numerous other occasions. Just like Clem, humans are prone to generalize fears as well.

For example, as a child when you were asked to try something new and challenging, you may have performed it badly. This could include experiences like talking in front of the class, trying a new game or sport or being asked a question that you didn't know the answer to but was obvious to your classmates. This may have caused you to be ridiculed. These uncomfortable experiences become embedded in your unconscious. At a later stage in life when you are offered the opportunity to try something new, you become triggered by the old experience and become fearful and reluctant to take a chance. As a result, you may be tempted to turn down the opportunity.

However, it isn't just personal experience that accounts for the array of things that you are fearful of in your life. Scientists have shown that the problem of fear is compounded, because you are also sensitive to the fears that you witness from observed events. In my own family, I have seen the fear of spiders passed down from mother to daughter through two or three generations. Your fearful reactions are made up of both individual and shared perceptions.

Types of Fear

There are many different types of fear. You may have experienced the fear of failure, the fear of success, the fear of public speaking or many other types. I believe the failure to escape from mind traps is traceable primarily to three key fears:

- Fear of ridicule
- Fear of repeating past mistakes
- Fear of the unknown

Fear of Ridicule

The fear of ridicule can create a massive obstacle in the process of change. As I discussed earlier, humans have a need for approval. It is an indication that they have a place within a group. The idea of social rejection creates strong negative emotions.

Allowing the fear of ridicule to hold you back is underpinned by a dangerous belief that the expectations of others are more important than the expectations you have for yourself. Often within a social group an identity becomes created for you. People among the group begin to believe that you should act in accordance with the group's identity. If you fall out of line, ridicule is often a means to remind you of your place. Ironically, the people in the group that are most likely to ridicule you have their own particular fear. If you succeed in changing, they fear you will invalidate the identity that they've created for themselves.

To make significant changes in your life, and escape the mind traps permanently, you have to stop caring so much about what the doubters may think and say (even if these doubters are very close to home). It is vital to stop restricting yourself because of other people's negative wishes and expectations of you. Forge your own path, and take strength from people you admire that have had the courage to change.

Fear of Repeating Past Mistakes

This is a topic I have personal experience with. I have found in my life that regardless of how old I am, there is often a part of me that says, "I should've figured this all out by now". I sense that I should've made more progress, and that I shouldn't have made so many mistakes. It is also a pattern I have noticed with virtually every client I have ever had as well. It seems to be an almost universal phenomenon that people feel they should have progressed more than they have. If you are behind in your progress toward an eventual goal, then "mistakes" can seem to rob you of crucial time.

Increasingly though, I have learned that these so-called "mistakes" are a vital part of the learning process. Despite having learned that, I can still find myself thinking that I don't want to repeat similar mistakes again. At times like that, I remind myself (as well as my clients) that the path to successful change isn't always a straight line. Taking a backward step occasionally is an inevitable part of progress. Mistakes will happen, they always do.

During the writing of this book for example, I have made countless errors. Not just in spelling and grammar, which are easily rectified, but also in the way I have set about completing it. I have to keep reminding myself that overcoming the fear involves accepting the disappointments and frustrations that happen along the journey.

My goal, like yours, is to do the best I can at any given moment. If you are held back by the fear of past mistakes, you need to consciously put aside any need to make things perfect. Trust that the more you focus on getting the job done, the more you will learn along the way. Success involves taking action, and moving out of or away from your trap. To keep focused and to alleviate the fear of past mistakes, keep the following quotation in mind: -

"Success seems to be connected with action. Successful people keep moving. They make mistakes, but they don't quit".
– Conrad Hilton

Understand that a big part of the "fear of past mistakes" is linked to not being prepared to take a step back. It is a type of impatience, a way of saying, "I want the change, but I am not prepared to wait". It's a reluctance to accept the truth that any worthwhile change almost inevitably involves sacrifice.

Fear of the Unknown

As I said earlier, the unconscious mind likes to form patterns and seeks coherence. Once it has grouped known experiences and known information into patterns, unknown experiences and unknown information can represent a challenge or threat to the existing paradigm. You unconsciously set parameters around what is safe and acceptable behavior, and that is why you often fear the unknown.

When confronted with the unknown, you don't know what to expect, you can't confidently predict the outcome of your behaviour, and a part of you starts to wonder if there might be negative consequences to adopting new behavior.

That pattern of thinking leads to the common experience of settling for what you have or what you get in your life. The problem is that once you settle for what you get in life, especially if you are settling for less than you deserve, it invariably feels as though something is being taken away from you. And it is!

What is being taken away from you is your value and your sense of self-worth. It becomes a downward spiral. If you value yourself less, you become less confident. If you are less confident, your performance drops, and your determination deteriorates. Ultimately, you start to lower your expectations.

To overcome fear of the unknown it is necessary to reverse the process. The first step is to raise the bar. Believe in your value and start to set higher expectations. When you expect more of yourself you develop the confidence to meet challenges face on. The pull toward a higher goal gives you the ability to tackle obstacles, in turn breeding confidence in the ability to take action in spite of fear. Your performance gradually improves, you start seeing results and your sense of self-worth starts to grow again.

What you experience at the other side of fear is never quite how you imagined it. Taking action and venturing into the unknown always leads to more opportunities and greater insight. The only way to make the unknown known is to confront the thing you fear most. Appreciate that deep inside of you, whatever happens, you will have the resources to be able to deal with it.

Dealing with Fear

Neuroscientists and psychologists have identified ways in which to defeat fear. It turns out that Jim Morrison, who I quoted at the beginning of the chapter, was spot on. It does not help to try to ignore or suppress a particular fear. Faced with the emotion of fear, the best thing you can do to overcome it is to expose yourself to the fear.

The problem with trying to suppress or ignore fear is that it brings into play the "ironic process". Simply put, the ironic process is summed up by the saying, - *"What you most resist, persists"*. In an online interview, Harvard University psychologist Daniel Wegner, an expert on the ironic process, describes it like this:

"When your conscious mind is under stress and preoccupied — a subconscious process devoted to guarding against the mistake slips through. Unwanted thoughts pop into the forefront of your mind".

Rather than trying to hide from the fear, the best option is to accept the challenge of confronting the fear head on. The most sensible way to do this is in a gradual and progressive way. Start by identifying what thoughts, emotions and physical sensations you experience in the fearful state. Whatever mind trap you are in, identify a step you can take to move you away from an unwanted behaviour or to move you towards a desirable goal.

Commit to that step 100 percent. Expose yourself to the fear of getting started. As soon as you take any sort of action in the direction of the fear, the level of the fear will start to subside. Soon, the unknown becomes known. And the thoughts, the emotions and the associated physical sensations become more and more bearable.

In the words of Arnold Schwarzenegger, *"When you go through hardships and decide not to surrender, that is strength"*.

Exercise 5:

Before you move on to part two of the book, read the following story, and write a list of at least 20 things you are grateful for.

A Story of Unbelievable Courage:

Immaculee Illagiza is a published author and highly sought after motivational speaker. She speaks all over the world and has been featured on mainstream U.S. television, including shows such as *60 minutes.* She has gained global recognition, having received the Mahatma Gandhi Reconciliation and Race Award in 2007. Most importantly, she is now happy, healthy and vibrant.

However, there was a time in her life that is almost unspeakable. In fact, when I first heard her story I found it terrifying almost beyond measure. This is a woman who lived through one of the worst atrocities imaginable, the Rwandan Genocide of 1994. This was a grotesque conflict that left 800,000 people slaughtered in just 100 days. The Tutsis, the country's minority tribe, were almost completely wiped out during that time.

The troubles started because the Tutsis were strongly resented by the Hutu tribe. The Tutsis had been seen as the elite and had better housing and better jobs. The Hutus were strongly encouraged to rise up against the Tutsis. With the promise of land and money, they became hell-bent on eradicating them.

Immaculee, a Tutsi living in a remote village, vividly remembers witnessing the first murder of a fellow villager across a field. What she saw was terrifying. It was a killing that was cold, brutal and raw. She watched helplessly as someone was hacked to death with a machete.

She knew it wouldn't be long until they were after her. On the advice of her father, she sought refuge with a friend of the family - a pastor - who ironically was part of the Hutu tribe. The pastor took pity on Immaculee and six other Tutsi women, and hid them in a tiny bathroom in a discreet corner of his house. The bathroom was tiny, measuring only 3 feet by 4 feet, but housed the women for a staggering 91 days.

Some of the Hutu tribe had seen the women enter the house but hadn't seen them leave. Dozens of them rallied together and stormed the house, determined to find and kill the sheltered women. Immaculee was petrified; her mouth became so dry she couldn't even swallow. The men armed with spears, machetes and nail-covered clubs - wanted blood. All that separated the women from the killers was a thin wall and the small bureau that the pastor had put in front of the entrance to the bathroom.

They were only inches away from certain death. Thoughts of what might happen ran through Immaculee's head. "Will they catch me? Where will they start cutting me? Will they rape me?"

One of the killers was someone she knew. He had been the family's handy-man. He called out for her by name. "I have killed 399 cockroaches", he said, "I want the 400th". Cockroaches is what the Hutus called the Tutsis. Hearing the man's voice felt like "dying alive" Immaculee later said.

Amazingly, all the women survived the ordeal. French troops intervened in the conflict, and the women fled the house and found refuge in one of their camps. Although she was now safe, Immaculee later discovered that her mother, father and two brothers had been killed.

Immaculee believes the Rwandans will never forget the atrocities but must learn how to forgive. She believes revenge only prolongs pain. She doesn't want the killers to cause what she calls – "luggage in her heart", so she won't hold on to the anger. She has forgiven a man responsible for killing two of her relatives. Asked if she would like to exact revenge on him, she said, - "I know in my heart that won't change anything. It won't bring back the people he killed".

Today, Immaculee is passionate about sharing the details of her experience. She feels compelled to spread her message. Her hope is that by bringing awareness to what happened, it will help bring a halt to future atrocities.

PART TWO

Chapter 10: Conquering the Demons - A Step-by-step Guide

As stated in the introduction to the book, there are definite steps to follow in order to escape a mind trap. Below are the key stages you'll need to go through to succeed. The first letter of each step spells out the acronym "ADORES". I encourage you to become someone who "adores" life rather than someone who just suffers it.

Awareness: -

"Between stimulus and response there is space. In that space is our power to choose our response"
– Viktor Frankl

The "A" in ADORES stands for awareness. This is the precursor of all successful change. In order to escape the mind traps, you need to observe what is going on, not just in the world around you, but in your own mind. Meaningful and lasting change requires lasting and consistent awareness. You need to become aware of how you are living on a day-to-day basis. This awareness relies on your ability to check-in with yourself, not just one time, but on a regular basis. For this reason, awareness has to become a practice, something that you do on a regular and consistent basis. Like all practices, the more you do it, the better it becomes.

There are many routes to awareness. A field that I am particularly familiar with is hypnotherapy, which is one of many modalities along with yoga and meditation, that have the same principle as their core. By slowing down the over-active cycle of automatic thought, you start to become aware that there is *a thinker behind your thinking.* With a growing awareness of the role you take in constructing your own model of the world, you can start to take conscious measures to avoid negative traps.

The key to effective awareness is to learn to observe your mind, thoughts, feelings and bodily sensations in a non-judgemental way. This allows you to notice what is happening internally and helps you observe how easy it is to drift into automatic and negative patterns of thought and behavior. As Viktor Frankl observes, you need to pause in that space between stimulus and response and take time to observe the patterns and loops that are operating inside of you.

Awareness also allows you to notice that thoughts can come and thoughts can go. In much the same way that a train can come in and leave the train station, practicing awareness will allow you to let your own thoughts come and go. You wouldn't take a train that is going in the wrong direction. Through awareness, you learn not to engage in a train of thought that leads to unnecessary pain. Being aware and attentive to the activity of your mind allows you to catch the negative patterns of thoughts and feelings before they take you over.

Renewed awareness paves the way to spend more time in the more productive "being" state rather than the less effective "outcome" state that I spoke of in Chapter 7. Through awareness you purposefully chose your actions and your reactions to the events of your life. You start to discover that there are many times when your brain is unnecessarily set to "alert" mode, making you overly cautious of dangers that are imaginary rather than real. Realizing this, allows you to relate to how things are in the present, and to move beyond your fearful states.

Awareness allows you to see thoughts for what they really are: mental events. You discover that you are not your thoughts and that your thoughts are not reality. Metaphorically, these thoughts are just an interpretation and description of one part of the elephant. You come to realize that your thoughts are a narrative, your story of the world as you have perceived it up to now.

How Can You Initiate Greater Awareness?

Initiating greater awareness starts by slowing down and minimizing the activity of the mind and body, so that the extraneous activity of the mind and body becomes more apparent. It involves willingness and courage to observe what is going on inside of you.

The process of real, long-lasting change requires you to stop, step back and observe what's going on. As we've already established, your mind spends a lot of time running on automatic. You go through your day doing the same things that you have done the previous day, the previous week, the previous month and even the last year. You allow the same anxieties, the same frustrations and the same feelings of guilt and shame to operate in an endless loop.

To get off the conveyor belt, you need to stop, allow yourself some mental and physical space, and take the time to reflect on what is working for you and what is holding you back. Give yourself as much time out as you can possibly afford. You deserve a break. If you find yourself saying, you don't have the time, or can't get away, you will know that these are just your normal demons trying to hold you back. Don't listen to them!

Everyone can find time if they plan for it. Even if you live a busy life, find an activity that you can drop and make sure you find time for honest reflection. If you deny yourself the time, then you deny yourself the opportunity for meaningful change. The choice is yours!

Once you've freed up some time, the next step is to do everything you can to remove yourself from your normal environment. Find somewhere peaceful, somewhere where you won't be disturbed and write down your thoughts, feelings and the physical sensations in your body.

Exercise 6:
Become aware of your traps and write them down.

Write down what you say to yourself that holds you back?
Write down what justification you use to keep yourself in old patterns of behavior?
Write down who or what you blame for these negative patterns of behavior?
Write down what excuses you make for not changing?

Become aware of the payoffs for old behavior.

Write down the benefits or payoffs you've gained from allowing yourself to remain stuck in the old ways. What or who has it allowed you to avoid? What part of your identity has it enabled you to reinforce? Notice whether you have received more attention from others for behaving in a negative way.

Become aware of the long-term cost of the mind trap.

How has the mind trap held you back in your life? What are you missing out on? What has been the impact to you personally and to the people around you? Think about these costs and how they affect you, both in the long term and on a daily basis.

Hold on to what you have written down. I encourage you to record it in a journal. At this stage, also become aware of the judgements you have made about yourself and the identity that you have adopted. Decide from now, that awareness is something that you will choose to cultivate and develop. Start researching which types of practices will suit you in growing self-awareness, and take the first steps to introduce that practice into your life.

Detachment:

"You've learned to judge, criticise and condemn yourself. No matter how hard anyone else has ever judged you, you judge yourself the hardest. In fact, you save the most severe standards, judgements, criticisms and punishments for yourself".
– Robert Holden

Becoming more aware will aid your path to mental freedom only if it goes hand-in-hand with growing self-compassion. Many of us have a tendency to be our own worst critics. We berate ourselves for our failures and wrongdoings. Internally, we verbally abuse ourselves in ways that would be considered unacceptable if this abuse was directed towards another.

Once you start to develop a growing self-awareness, the next step to long-lasting change is to break these negative cycles and thought patterns. This involves the ability to detach from negative elements of your own story.

In my experience, people truly are their own worst enemies. In consultations with clients I have heard phrases like "I was such an idiot", "I'm such a fuck up" or "it's my fault". Although this is an over-simplification, I believe much of it derives from the dominant psychological picture of man during the 20th century. The Freudian theory that says we are determined by forces from our past causes us to become fixated on childhood trauma that never truly gets resolved. We then spend our adult lives trying to fix ourselves. It is what I deem a "broken model of man", and it is erroneous.

Like all humans, you and I are imperfect. Once you accept that, it opens up the door for change. There is a world of difference between imperfect and broken. Accepting imperfection allows for adjustments, alterations, improvements and change. Believing that you are broken and beyond repair leads to the crippling closed mind I referred to in Chapter 7.

Ironically, the judgements you make about your routine behaviour and routine thought patterns are the very things that keep you caught in the trap. These judgements reinforce a negative identity which was made up in the first place! It is time to detach from this negative self concept.

Detach from Judgement

"The highest form of human intelligence is to observe your-self without judgement"
- Krishnamurti

There are two major judgements that people make about themselves: judgements about lack and judgements about excess. Judgements about lack include statements like, "I'm not attractive enough, rich enough, intelligent enough or strong enough". It doesn't matter what resource these statements refer to. They are all about lack and are underpinned by the generalized belief that who you are is not enough.

The reverse of judgements about lack is judgements about excess. Typical statements might include, "I'm too fat, I'm too clumsy, or my personality is too addictive". All of these judgements are a result of comparisons. You compare yourself to an individual or group of people, to your former self, or to an idealized standard.

Whichever one it is, there is an easy way to start detaching from these judgements. Listen to the negative statements you say about your-self and delete justifications from your thought process, especially the ones that start with the word "because".

Here are examples of what I mean:

- I am overweight because of my genetics.
- I am broke because of my upbringing.
- I smoke because I am stressed.
- I won't accept the challenge because I am afraid.

When you start dropping these justifications, these thoughts become:

- I am overweight.
- I am broke.

- I smoke.
- I won't accept the challenge.

If you read the first group and second group of sentences aloud, you will feel that the second group has less hold over you.

Now add a new statement that allows you to stay optimistic and open.

I suggest the following:

"This is only temporary. Through perseverance I will achieve the results I desire"

The new statements would look something like this:

- I am overweight. This is only temporary. Through perseverance I will have the body I desire.
- I am broke. This is only temporary. Through perseverance I will achieve the wealth I desire.
- I smoke. This is only temporary. Through perseverance I will regain the healthy body I desire.
- I won't accept the challenge. This is only temporary. Through perseverance I will gain the confidence I desire.

I advise you to note these revised beliefs in a journal. Keep them as new beliefs that you can refer to and use again and again.

Detach from Your Story

As was pointed out earlier, one of the key features of the left side of the brain is its ability to create stories or a narrative of your life. It is an incredibly useful ability that helps keep you sane and functioning in the real world. It is however just your story. When you are absorbed in the drama of the story, it feels very real. For the story to make sense, you create internal cohesion to the narrative, leaving alternative explanations abandoned or ignored.

The truth is that once you take a step back, and bring awareness to your story, you see the flaws in the narrative. Only then can you begin to re-invent and re-create the next chapter of your life. Much as the inspirational figures in the first part of this book have done, you can take charge of what happens next. Rather than being the actor playing out a bit part, you become the director of the show. The narrative of the story begins to change dramatically once the decision has been made to write your own script.

Openness:

"Limits, like fears, are often just an illusion"
– Michael Jordan.

Once you have released yourself from the drama of judgement and stories, it is time to open your mind to new possibilities. Openness is the "O" in ADORES.

As you have learned from the discussions of the left side of the brain, there is a tendency to compare present behaviour to past behavior when considering whether you are likely to be successful in implementing change. This creates limits to what you think you are capable of achieving. This approach is far too restrictive and narrow.

It is a closed approach to thinking that is counter-productive to overcoming the obstacles to your progress. Awareness and detachment prepare the path for change, but openness allows you to walk through the door.

It sounds obvious, but when you are trying to escape mind traps to initiate tangible and permanent change, you have to do something different from what you have done so far. You have to be *open* to new ways of thinking, feeling, sensing and behaving. You have to interrupt the existing patterns and loops playing in your mind.

Realize that being open is an attitude you can adopt. But more importantly, it is also a skill. As a skill, being open has specific qualities that you can learn and develop.

Openness starts with focusing on what is **possible** rather than what is probable. It involves going beyond what is in front of you, or already inside of you. It means scanning for information outside of your existing field of vision or field of consciousness, and identifying new stimuli that brings you closer to your goal. It means being receptive to alternatives, observing and learning from other explanations, actions and ways of looking at the world that have been effective for people who have successfully walked the path you are looking to walk.

An open mind spots opportunity. It feeds off the belief that if there are other people out there who can make life-changing decisions, against all odds, then you can too. That is why stories of success are so important in building the confidence and belief you need to forge forward. Actively seeking out other's experiences, and keeping them in mind, will help you speed up the process of change.

Exercise 7:

This exercise will help you develop an open mind. Select a mind trap that you identified at the beginning of the book.

Ask yourself the following questions, and note your answers in your journal:

What are some alternative ways of thinking about your current situation?

Who do you know who has achieved the change that you are looking to make?

What do you admire about those who have successfully changed this area of their life?

What opportunities will open up for you as you escape the mind trap?

What stories inspire you the most?

What compromises and sacrifices are you willing to make to be free?

Start to reflect on others who've made the changes you are looking to make. Imagine what would happen if you were to put in place the beliefs and behaviors that allowed these people to move forward in their lives.

Once you have opened your mind, it is time to re-focus your energies on what you truly want.

Refocus:

"The secret of change is to focus all of your energy, not on fighting the old, but on building the new"
— Socrates.

There are expression in the English language that make me shudder every time I hear them, "Same old, same old", and "Same shit, different day". What I find challenging with both of these responses is that they imply and reinforce inevitability in life. It's as if life is destined to follow a path of predictability and tedium as it unfolds from one unsatisfying experience to the next.

Where these expressions miss the point is in their lack of appreciation that life is dynamic, not static. They fail to recognise that change is an inevitable part of life. Just as everything in nature undergoes change, the mind is in a constant state of flux. It is either working to reinforce old perceptions and old ways of thinking, or it is making new connections and new patterns.

As Buddha pointed out, *"Your life is the creation of your mind"*. How you direct your attention has a massive impact on what shows up in your life. If you choose, you can resign yourself to the inertia of unsupportive routines and behaviours. In effect, what you'll be doing is giving tacit consent to the mind trap. You can live life unconsciously, and let the patterns of the past play out in an endless loop (like putting the needle into the groove of a worn out record and playing the "same old, same old" tune over and over again).

Alternatively, you can make the choice to live more consciously, understanding that you're recreating your life each and every day. If you choose to recreate your life, you need to know where to start. And the best way to re-focus your attention is to consider what you actually want. Start by re-focusing your attention on solutions.

Focusing on what you want - the solution - is a relatively new approach. Traditionally there has been a tendency, especially amongst therapists, of trying to solve problems by focusing on the problem. However, there are now schools of thought that suggest that the way to overcome a problem is to take the focus away from the problem, and refocus attention on what is going right.

Books such as, 'Now, Discover Your Strengths' by Marcus Buckingham and Donald Clifton, 'The Element' by Ken Robinson, and 'The Solutions Focus' by Paul Z Jackson and Mark McKergow, reflect this change in mindset. The emerging paradigm shift encourages you to look at what you do well and expand on it, rather than focusing on what you do badly.

These writers encourage you to build momentum by amplifying your strengths, and taking attention away from the things you don't do well. (This lies at the heart of re-focusing). As Mark McKergow points out, analyzing the problem makes you an expert on the problem, but not on the solution. I couldn't agree more, and I believe refocusing on solutions and not problems is an integral part of escaping mind traps.

In order to illustrate the concept, I draw an analogy from my time coaching tennis some years ago. One player was throwing away too many points as a result of hitting a high percentage of services into the net. His concern was on how to stop hitting the ball into the net.

What he was doing by asking himself that question was focusing more attention on the net (the problem), and less on where the ball is meant to go (the solution). He started to improve when he shifted his attention to where he wanted the ball to land rather than avoiding the net. Put simply, he started to focus on what he wanted, rather than on what he didn't want.

Exercise 8:

Take some time to decide what you ultimately want. Allow your-self to refocus.

Ask your-self, what lies at the other side of the mind trap?
What is it that you aspire to? What is your bigger purpose?

Once you have re-focused on what you want, it's time to do something about it. You have to expose your-self to your deepest fears.

Exposure:

"The secret of getting ahead is getting started. The secret of getting started is breaking your complex, overwhelming task into small manageable tasks, and then starting on the first one"
- Mark Twain.

Exposure is about stepping out of your existing pattern of thought and behavior, and experimenting with the new and unknown. Taking that first step is often the obstacle that holds you back from wholesale change. You have to give your-self first-hand experience of the alternative way of thinking or behaving if you are ever going to make the more desirable alternative a reality.

The experience that you gain by taking any action in the direction of your new goal is crucial. It is only through action and experience that your confidence to implement change develops. With each new experience that you witness in the right direction, confidence compounds. Once you take a brave step for the first time, your belief that you can conquer it again more than doubles.

However, exposure is not always about throwing yourself in at the deep end. If you know that you have the confidence to immerse yourself in a new experience, then throwing yourself 'all-in' is an option. Often this approach is counter-productive. It can lead to burn out and can be tantamount to overturning the elephant with brute force. I believe it is more appropriate to expose yourself to new experiences incrementally. The more critical question becomes how often you adopt the new behaviour not how deeply do you immerse your-self in the new experience. Good habits are formed through frequent and consistent exposure.

To demonstrate what I mean, let me reverse engineer a commonplace bad habit. Take someone who smokes. As a child, chances are they were exposed to smoking in gradual stages. They weren't asked to sit and smoke a pack of 20 in one sitting, but were encouraged to pursue the new habit with a few puffs on their first cigarette. If they were subsequently exposed to that experience on a regular and consistent basis, the degree to which they smoked increased until the new habit was formed.

Slow and Steady Wins the Race

When a mind trap has prevented you from pursuing what you want, there is no need to try and achieve the new goal all at once. I'm a great believer in breaking down the goal into micro stages. There is a riddle that asks, 'How do you eat an elephant?' The answer is one bite at a time. That is how to achieve what you want – in bite sized pieces. The illusion of overnight success is just that, an illusion. The mind needs to adapt and adjust in order to incorporate new loops and new patterns.

As Aristotle said, "*We are what we repeatedly do. Excellence, then, is not an act, but a habit*". This is how you set up new patterns in your mind. You groove a new behavior or thought into the left side of your brain, establishing new neurological circuits that create new loops. From a neurological point of view, every time a circuit is utilized, it takes less external stimulus for it to run the circuit again. The new activity becomes "normalized" and starts to establish the new habit.

Taking that First Step

There are two big challenges you may face when taking your first step. You either view the first small step as futile in relation to the monumental task you face, or you are intimidated by the discomfort, awkwardness or 'suffering' that first step takes.

If your challenge is that you see the task ahead as too monumental, I encourage you to keep in mind the quotation by Martin Luther King: "*Faith is taking the first step even when you don't see the whole staircase*". Remind your-self that anything of worth that you have accomplished in your life took time. How that accomplishment panned out evolved in a way that you couldn't necessarily have foreseen from the outset.

With this in mind you can appreciate that although you may not know exactly *how* you will break free from your mind trap, you are certain that you will. Have faith; the how will reveal itself to you as you go through the process.

Maybe your biggest obstacle to taking the first step is your resistance to the perceived suffering you will endure during the process of change. At some point you have to accept that no meaningful change will occur without a degree of compromise, sacrifice or even discomfort. The inability to accept hardship and suffering in life is a huge part of what keeps you enslaved in mind traps. As Dr. Stephen Briers points out in his book '*Psychobabble*', "In *Asian cultures suffering is regarded as a precondition of growth*". I think it is a valid premise. No meaningful change ever occurs without a degree of sacrifice. As Jim Rohn once asked, "*What would you rather suffer from, the pain of discipline or the pain of regret?*" Be prepared to go through some initial discomfort, and you will be rewarded ten-fold.

Exercise 9:

Ask your-self this one question:

What are you willing to give up to free your-self from the mind trap?

Shift:

The final part of the ADORES system that allows you to make progress toward escaping the mind trap is realizing that in time it is possible to make big strides in the direction you want to go. It is an appreciation that you can make significant shifts in your progress.

But these shifts are not an activity, they are a concept. By being aware that shifts happen, your willingness to persevere in the pursuit of meaningful change will intensify. You start to accept the minor set-backs in your pursuit of meaningful change, safe in the knowledge that quantum changes can happen, once you are open to them.

As I learned from my book mentor, best-selling author Raymond Aaron, changes can be of two types: transactional and transformational. Often, the progress you make will be small and feel inconsequential; these are the transactional changes in your life that move you forward inch by inch.

Transformational changes, however, are those that take you to a new level. These changes create a shift in your consciousness that allow you to make massive progress towards achieving your goals. They occur when you pay closer attention to the context of all your thoughts, behaviours and actions; when something, or someone, enables you to look at, and experience, the bigger picture. These transformational changes occur only when you allow your paradigms to change. Your paradigms, or your models of the world, are based on a set of assumptions, ideas, values and practices that create your way of perceiving reality.

The word paradigm means example. It is the examples that you follow to navigate your world that have the biggest impact on how you live your life.

If you can't find examples of how to escape the mind traps within your own experience, then I encourage you to actively seek out the examples of others in order to create the shift. You can find these examples either by seeking out inspiring stories of transformation, similar to the ones in this book; or you can find a coach or mentor who will provide you with examples that will help you break free.

The greatest changes of all come when you change your paradigm. As you shift the core beliefs that link your minor beliefs together your understanding and awareness of reality changes irreversibly. You can witness this by reflecting on your life so far. If you think back to times in your life when your core beliefs were shifted, you'll see how the minor beliefs associated with it, were instantly changed.

One of the most powerful shifts for many people comes during early childhood. As a child you maybe caught Mom or Dad sneaking into your bedroom on Christmas Eve. It then dawned on you that Santa Claus was not real. Once you realize that Santa is not a guy in a red-and-white suit that flies around the world, your beliefs about the presents under the tree, the half-eaten mince pies and the magical reindeer are all reversed. I use this example not to remind you of childhood trauma, but to demonstrate that once a core belief is reversed, it has the effect of reversing all the minor beliefs that underpin that story.

Perhaps the story you have told yourself is that your life is different. In your life story, you have convinced your-self it is not possible to escape your mind traps. You may also believe that your circumstances, and the pressures you face, make it impossible for you to change.

Know that this is the story that you have made-up for your-self, and it is as imaginary as the story of Santa Claus. Allow your-self to experience a different reality. Take the first steps in breaking free from your mind traps, and allow the shifts to happen in your own life. Seek out the inspiring examples of others. But more importantly, make your own life an inspiring example.

Realize that you do not have to be defined by your past. You are free to break free from your mind traps whenever you want. And to remind you of that fact, I leave you with this thought provoking quote:

"You don't have to live your life forever defined by the damaging things that have happened to you. You are unique, you are irreplaceable; what lies within you can never be truly colonized, contorted or taken away. Your light never goes out"
- Eleanor Longdon

Bonuses:

For access to the following four bonuses and much more, please visit www.escapethemindtrap.com

1. An easy meditation to clear your mind
    - Helps to relieve stress
    - Clear the mind in minutes
    - Can be done virtually anywhere and at any time

2. A guide to creative visualization
    - Empowers you to envision a clearer picture of the life you want to live
    - Helps to purge unwanted thoughts from the past

3. Audio download of an interview with a self-made millionaire who explains how he successfully escaped the "money mind trap"
    - Learn the classic traps and how to escape them
    - Learn from the paradigms of the wealthy

4. Audio download from a leading nutritionist on freeing yourself from "dieting mind traps"
    - Learn why diets are not the answer
    - Discover new ways to think about the food you eat
    - Learn how to feel more in control of what you eat

Lightning Source UK Ltd.
Milton Keynes UK
UKOW03f0806020114

223844UK00002B/83/P